MW00352294

Eat That Frog!
ACTION WORKBOOK

Other Books by Brian Tracy

Eat That Frog!

Maximum Achievement

Advanced Selling Strategies

The 100 Absolutely Unbreakable Laws of Business Success

The 21 Success Secrets of Self-Made Millionaires

Focal Point

Victory!

Create Your Own Future

Goals!

TurboStrategy

Be a Sales Superstar

Hire and Keep the Best People

Get Paid More and Promoted Faster

Change Your Thinking, Change Your Life

Million Dollar Habits

Time Power

Getting Rich Your Own Way

TurboCoach

The Psychology of Selling

Something for Nothing

The Art of Closing the Sale

Crunch Point

The Way to Wealth

Eat That Frog!

ACTION WORKBOOK

Brian Tracy

BK

Berrett–Koehler Publishers, Inc.
a BK Life book

Copyright © 2017 by Brian Tracy

All rights reserved. No part of this publication may be reproduced, distributed, or transmitted in any form or by any means, including photocopying, recording, or other electronic or mechanical methods, without the prior written permission of the publisher, except in the case of brief quotations embodied in critical reviews and certain other noncommercial uses permitted by copyright law. For permission requests, write to the publisher, addressed "Attention: Permissions Coordinator," at the address below.

Berrett-Koehler Publishers, Inc.
1333 Broadway, Suite 1000,
Oakland, CA 94612-1921
Tel: (510) 817-2277   Fax: (510) 817-2278   www.bkconnection.com

Ordering Information

Quantity sales. Special discounts are available on quantity purchases by corporations, associations, and others. For details, contact the "Special Sales Department" at the Berrett-Koehler address above.

Individual sales. Berrett-Koehler publications are available through most bookstores. They can also be ordered directly from Berrett-Koehler: Tel: (800) 929-2929; Fax: (802) 864-7626; www.bkconnection.com

Orders for college textbook/course adoption use. Please contact Berrett-Koehler: Tel: (800) 929-2929; Fax: (802) 864-7626.

Orders by U.S. trade bookstores and wholesalers. Please contact Ingram Publisher Services, Tel: (800) 509-4887; Fax: (800) 838-1149; E-mail: customer.service@ingrampublisherservices.com; or visit www.ingrampublisherservices.com/Ordering for details about electronic ordering.

Berrett-Koehler and the BK logo are registered trademarks of Berrett-Koehler Publishers, Inc.

Printed in the United States of America

Berrett-Koehler books are printed on long-lasting acid-free paper. When it is available, we choose paper that has been manufactured by environmentally responsible processes. These may include using trees grown in sustainable forests, incorporating recycled paper, minimizing chlorine in bleaching, or recycling the energy produced at the paper mill.

ISBN: 978-1-5230-8470-8
22 21 20 19 18 17   6 5 4 3 2 1

Project manager: Susan Geraghty
Designer: Paula Goldstein
Cover designer: Irene Morris Design
Copyeditor: Michele Jones
Composition: Westchester Publishing Services
Proofreader: Sophia Ho

To my remarkable daughter Catherine,
an amazing girl with a wonderful mind
and an incredible future lying before her

Contents

How to Use This Book   ix

Introduction: Meet Shane   xi

1   Set the Table   1

2   Plan Every Day in Advance   9

3   Apply the 80/20 Rule to Everything   18

4   Consider the Consequences   21

5   Practice Creative Procrastination   25

6   Use the ABCDE Method Continually   34

7   Focus on Key Result Areas   38

8   Apply the Law of Three   43

9   Prepare Thoroughly Before You Begin   49

10 Take It One Oil Barrel at a Time   51

11 Upgrade Your Key Skills   55

12 Identify Your Key Constraints   59

13 Put the Pressure on Yourself   68

14 Motivate Yourself into Action   73

15 Technology Is a Terrible Master   78

16 Technology Is a Wonderful Servant   83

17   Focus Your Attention   87

18   Slice and Dice the Task   91

19   Create Large Chunks of Time   95

20   Develop a Sense of Urgency   102

21   Single Handle Every Task   109

Conclusion: Putting It All Together   112

Digital Resources   116

Learning Resources of Brian Tracy International   117

About the Author   121

How to Use This Book

Thanks for picking up this book. If you're working through *Eat That Frog!*—or just living a normal life—you know that there's simply never enough time to do everything that needs doing. As much as you might keep alive the idea that you'll eventually get caught up, you won't. All you can do to get control over your life is change the way you spend your time—shifting it away from some things, and toward others. While you can't do everything, you can always do *something*.

This workbook is set up to help you take action. Packed full of prompts for self-reflection and useful organizational tips and tools, its aim is to give you everything you need to think on paper and bring about real improvements in performance. It just might change your life.

Besides exercises that align with the key principles from *Eat That Frog!*, the workbook periodically includes the example of Shane, a narrative character introduced in the following section, working through her own struggles with procrastination and productivity.

You'll also find a Digital Resources page in the back of the workbook with a link to free charts and graphs from the chapter exercises. Print them out and use them again and again. You may also use the workbook in conjunction with the *Eat That Frog! Video Training Program,* which presents each chapter of the *Eat That Frog!* book and invites you to do the exercises in the workbook before moving on to the next lesson.

Without further ado, take action. Get more done. *Eat that frog!*

Introduction: Meet Shane

Like many people, Shane finds herself at a crossroads in her professional life. She's a middle manager at a reputable firm and likes her job well enough. She has good health care, enjoys her coworkers, and makes enough money to pay her bills, take the occasional vacation, and save a little on the side. But pushing papers isn't her real passion—chocolate is. For years, she's been concocting confections in her home kitchen, tweaking recipes and testing them out on an all-too-willing focus group of family and friends. Recently, she decided to take her treats to the masses—or at least to the weekend farmers market in her neighborhood. She rented out a corner of a commercial kitchen in the warehouse district, where she spends some evenings preparing and packaging the treats she'll hawk every Sunday. At the market, she gets a great response—and even has some loyal, repeat customers—but the haul she brings in isn't nearly enough to let her quit her day job. She's convinced that if she really wants to grow her business and be successful in the long term, it will really help to get her MBA. But how will she find the time to do it all, and also have some semblance of a personal life? In the face of so many competing priorities, she finds herself procrastinating—instead of moving surely and confidently toward her goals, she waffles, gets lost in social media streams, and is often unfocused. Papers are strewn across her desk, and the tasks just keep mounting. If she's going to keep her head above water, she needs to make some changes.

Set the Table

Goals are the fuel in the furnace of achievement. The bigger your goals and the clearer they are, the more excited you become about achieving them. The more you think about your goals, the greater become your inner drive and your desire to accomplish them.

1. With written goals, you'll be far more productive and efficient than people who just carry goals around in their heads. Use the space below to make a list of 10 goals you want to accomplish in the next year. Write your goals as though a year has already passed and they are now a reality. If you have trouble getting them down on your own, consider talking to your boss or a trusted confidant.

Goal 1: _____

_____

_____

Goal 2: _____

_____

_____

Goal 3: _____

_____

_____

Goal 4: _____

_____

_____

Goal 5: _____

_____

_____

Goal 6: _____

_____

_____

Goal 7: _____

_____

_____

Goal 8: _____

_____

_____

Goal 9: _____

_____

_____

Goal 10: _____

_____

_____

2. Review your list of 10 goals and select the one goal that, if you achieved it within 24 hours, would have the greatest positive impact on your life.

   Write it down on the line provided. Set a deadline. Then make a list of everything that you can think of that you can do to achieve that goal.

   Finally, take action. Do something every day that moves you at least one step toward that goal.

Goal: _____

Deadline: _____

1. _____

   _____

   _____

2. _____

   _____

   _____

3. _____

   _____

   _____

4. _____

   _____

   _____

5. _____

   _____

   _____

6. _____

_____

_____

7. _____

_____

_____

8. _____

_____

_____

9. _____

_____

_____

10. _____

_____

_____

3. Organize your list of activities by priority and sequence. Create a checklist, where each task appears in the order it needs to be done. Take some time to get this right— what needs to be done first and what can wait, what needs to be done before other activities can be completed. Then resolve to do something *right now* toward achieving your goal.

☐ _____

_____

☐ _____

_____

☐ _____

_____

☐ _____

_____

☐ _____

_____

☐ _____

_____

☐ _____

_____

☐ _____

_____

☐ _____

_____

- [ ] _____
  _____
- [ ] _____
  _____
- [ ] _____
  _____
- [ ] _____
  _____
- [ ] _____
  _____
- [ ] _____
  _____
- [ ] _____
  _____
- [ ] _____
  _____
- [ ] _____
  _____
- [ ] _____
  _____
- [ ] _____
  _____

1. Work out a plan for achieving your goal. Use the space on this page to draw a series of boxes and circles, with lines and arrows showing the relationships among the tasks. Color code items if it helps. You will be amazed at how much more achievable your goal seems when it's broken down into smaller tasks. Here is how Shane visualized her goals and tasks:

Shane's Goal and Tasks

2

Plan Every Day
in Advance

Think on paper, and plan every day in advance. You'll feel more powerful and competent. You'll get more done faster than you thought possible. You'll be unstoppable!

1. Planning your day in advance takes only a few minutes, but can save you hours. Always work from a list. First, make a *master list*. Think of this as the wide end of the funnel— the place where you capture every idea and every new task or responsibility that comes up.

1. _____

_____

_____

2. _____

_____

_____

3. _____

_____

_____

4. _____

_____

_____

5. _____

_____

_____

6. _____

_____

_____

7. _____

_____

_____

8. _____

_____

_____

9. _____

_____

_____

10. _____

_____

_____

2. At the end of each month, prepare a *monthly list* of items that you plan to tackle in the month ahead. Pull from your master list. What has to be done first? What comes next? Start with the end in mind and work backward.

1. _____

   _____

   _____

2. _____

   _____

   _____

3. _____

   _____

   _____

4. _____

   _____

   _____

5. _____

   _____

   _____

6. _____

   _____

   _____

7. _____

_____

_____

8. _____

_____

_____

9. _____

_____

_____

10. _____

_____

_____

3. Next, create a *weekly list.* This list may change as you go through the current week.

1. _____

_____

_____

2. _____

_____

_____

3. _____

_____

_____

4. _____

_____

_____

5. _____

_____

_____

6. _____

_____

_____

7. _____

_____

_____

8. _____

_____

_____

9. _____

_____

_____

10. _____

_____

_____

4. If your master list is the wide end of a funnel, your *daily list* is the narrow end. On your daily list, include specific activities that you're going to accomplish on the following day. As you complete them, tick them off the list as a sign of visible progress.

☐ _____

_____

_____

☐ _____

_____

_____

☐ _____

_____

_____

☐ _____

_____

_____

☐ _____

_____

_____

☐ _____

_____

_____

☐ _____

3

Apply the 80/20 Rule to Everything

Resist the temptation to clear up small things first. Small things are like rabbits; they multiply continually. Get in the habit of tackling the "vital few" before you attend to the "trivial many."

1. The things you choose to do repeatedly eventually become habits—habits that can be hard to break. If you prioritize low-value tasks, that becomes a habit—but so does prioritizing high-value tasks. So, what are you going to make a habit of doing more?

_____

_____

_____

What are you going to make a habit of doing less?

_____

_____

_____

What are you going to start doing?

_____

_____

_____

What are you going to stop doing altogether?

_____

_____

_____

2. Productive people discipline themselves to start on the most important task before them. They force themselves to eat that frog, no matter how slimy or smelly it might be. Take some time, right now, to work on your highest-value activity. Take some action—any action—immediately. Really. Put this book down and go *do something*. Don't worry. I'll wait.

Shane settled on her two most important goals: get her MBA and grow her chocolate business to the point where she can quit her day job. Toward these ends, Shane started planning out her days in advance—each second that she wasn't performing necessary duties at her firm was devoted to working on her schoolwork and getting her chocolates in front of new potential customers. She also started making a habit of getting up a couple hours early to get a jump on her reading.

4

Consider the Consequences

The clearer you are about your future goals, the sharper present priorities come into focus. Accept the fact that there will never be enough time to do everything. Then do first things first, and second things not at all.

1. Successful people have a strong orientation toward the future. Their attitude toward time—their "time horizon"—influences choices and behavior in the short term. What are your goals? And where do you see yourself? Use this chart to map out your 5-year, 10-year, and 20-year goals in the areas of business success, financial independence, family/relationships, and health/fitness.

	Business Success	Financial Independence	Family and Relationships	Health and Fitness
In 5 years?				
In 10 years?				
In 20 years?				

2. And where are you right now? Take a minute to grade yourself on a 1-10 scale in each area (10 being the best). Put a dot on each score and connect them for a sense of your current life. (The goal is to have a perfect diamond.)

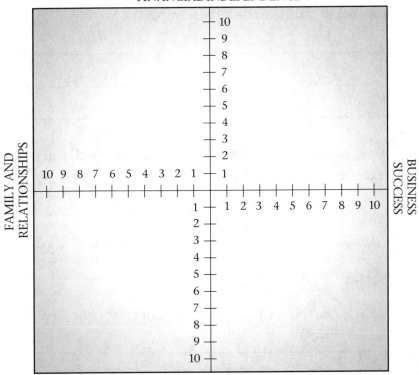

FINANCIAL INDEPENDENCE

FAMILY AND RELATIONSHIPS

BUSINESS SUCCESS

HEALTH AND FITNESS

Where are you strongest? Weakest?

_____

_____

_____

_____

_____

3. There will never be enough time to do everything you have to do. All you can hope for is to be on top of your most important responsibilities. Based on where you are and where you hope to go:

What are your highest-value activities—those frogs you have to eat to make the largest impact?

_____

_____

_____

What can you and *only* you do, that if done well, will make a real difference?

_____

_____

_____

What is the most valuable use of your time *right now*?

_____

_____

_____

5

Practice Creative Procrastination

Everybody procrastinates, but creative procrastination can change your life. Deliberately and consciously procrastinate on low-value tasks. Eat the biggest, ugliest frogs before you even think about dealing with the tadpoles.

1. You can get your time and your life under control only as much as you discontinue lower-value activities. To set priorities—what you do more of and sooner—you must set posteriorities, or those things that you do less of and later, if at all. Think about how you spend your day, week, or month. Which activities are the true priorities? Which ones should you do later, if at all? Pick a time (day, week, month, year) and then write down your priorities and posteriorities on the following diagram.

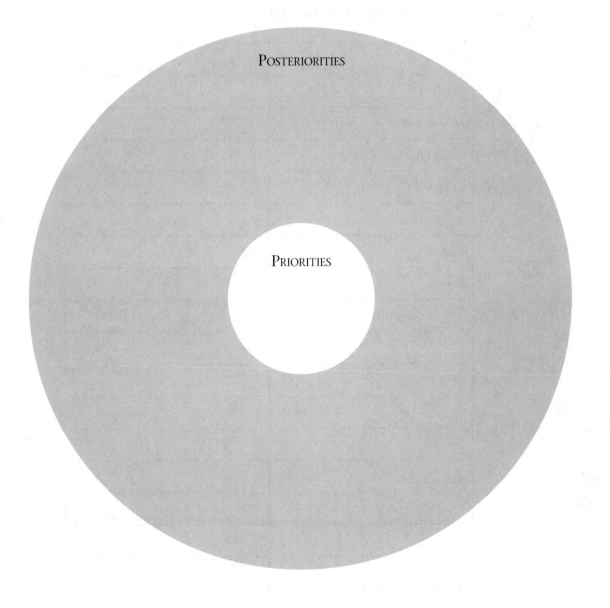

2. Look at your life outside of work. Which activities do you find yourself spending a lot of time on, with little value added to your life? Using the chart, lay out the amount of time you spend on different activities daily. Use the blank spaces to make the chart your own.

Activity	Hours Spent Daily
Watching TV	
Internet surfing	
Favorite hobby	
On phone	
With family	
Reading	
Exercise	

3. Look at the most time-consuming activities in the chart. Do they help you become more successful or otherwise enhance your quality of life in a meaningful way? Scrutinize each of your personal and work activities and evaluate it based on your current situation. Select at least one activity to abandon right now—or at least deliberately put off until your more important goals have been achieved. You must put something down if you're going to pick something else up!

4. Practice "zero-based" thinking. Ask yourself: "Knowing what I know now, is there anything I am doing today that I wouldn't get into again today if I had it to do over?"

Key Question: "Knowing what I now know, is there anything I am doing today that I wouldn't get into again today if I had it to do over?"

1. Is there any relationship, business or personal, that I wouldn't get into again today?

    • _____

    • _____

    • _____

2. Are there any products I would not start offering/selling again today, knowing what I now know?

    • _____

    • _____

    • _____

3. Are there any services I wouldn't start offering today?

    • _____

    • _____

    • _____

4. Are there any markets I wouldn't get into again today if I had it to do over?

    • _____

- _____

- _____

5. Are there any customers I would not solicit or take on again today, knowing what I now know?

   - _____

   - _____

   - _____

6. Are there any sales processes or methods I wouldn't start using today, knowing what I now know?

   - _____

   - _____

   - _____

7. Are there any staff members I would not hire, promote, or assign to a particular task if I had it to do over again today?

   - _____

   - _____

   - _____

8. Are there any channels of distribution that I would not start using if I was starting over today?

   - _____

   - _____

   - _____

9. Are there any business processes or methods in my company that I wouldn't start using if I had it to do over?

- _____
- _____
- _____

10. Are there any advertising or marketing methods or expenses that I wouldn't get into again, knowing what I now know?

- _____
- _____
- _____

11. Are there any sales offers that I wouldn't get into again if I had them to do over?

- _____
- _____
- _____

12. Is there anything in my current strategy that I would change or discontinue if I had it to do over again today?

- _____
- _____
- _____

13. Is there any investment of time, money, or emotion that I wouldn't get into again today?

- _____

- _____

- _____

14. Is there anything to do with my health, fitness, diet, or lifestyle that I wouldn't start again today?

- _____

- _____

- _____

15. What actions am I going to take, or stop taking, as a result of this exercise?

- _____

- _____

- _____

16. What one action am I going to take immediately?

- _____

6

Use the ABCDE Method Continually

If you're thinking on paper, you're already in the minority. The more effort you put into planning and setting priorities before you start, the more important things you'll do and the faster you'll do them. Using the ABCDE Method can, all by itself, make you one of the most efficient and effective people in your field.

1. What do you have to do today? Take five minutes to write down everything, from main priorities to things that wouldn't kill you if they slipped through the cracks.

_____

_____

_____

_____

_____

_____

_____

_____

_____

_____

_____

_____

_____

_____

_____

_____

_____

_____

2. Before you do anything on your list, prioritize! Return to your list and mark each item according to the ABCDE Method:

A—Mark each item that is very important and *must* be done today—the real frogs in your life—with an *A*. If you have more than one A task, prioritize them (A-1, A-2, etc.).

B—Mark any task that you *should* do—meaning something that would have minor consequences if it didn't get finished—with a *B*. The B's are the tadpoles that might result in inconvenience, but won't cause any major damage.

C—C's are the "nice-to-dos." It might be nice to take a break with a colleague or get some of your personal tasks done during work hours, but they're not really necessary—they don't affect your work life at all.

D—Delegate, delegate, delegate. Anything *you* don't need to do—that someone else could just as easily finish—mark with a *D*. Doing so will free up more time for you to knock out those A's.

E—Mark everything that you can eliminate altogether with an *E*. Maybe you keep doing certain things out of habit rather than for any real reason. Whatever the case, if it doesn't make any real difference, eliminate it.

More often than she'd care to admit, Shane found herself glancing up to see that a whole hour had passed while she scrolled through her unending Twitter feed. Not only was this time poorly spent, but the constant barrage of media made her anxious, contributing to a general sense of unease. She decided to eliminate all social media time that wasn't directly related to boosting her brand or productivity.

7

Focus on Key Result Areas

Know why you're on the payroll. Identify the key result areas of your work. Know that your weakest key result area is the one holding you back. Don't justify, rationalize, or defend your weaknesses. Identify them clearly and work to improve. Just think! You may be only one critical skill away from top performance.

1. The starting point of high performance is identifying your key result areas—those things for which you are entirely responsible, that are wholly under your control, and that, when completed, impact the work of others. Take a minute to write down your five to seven key result areas.

Key Result Area 1:

_____

_____

_____

Key Result Area 2:

_____

_____

_____

Key Result Area 3:

_____

_____

_____

Key Result Area 4:

_____

_____

_____

Key Result Area 5:

_____

_____

_____

Key Result Area 6:

_____

_____

_____

Key Result Area 7:

_____

_____

_____

2. A lot of the time, poor performance drives procrastination. People avoid the jobs where they've struggled in the past. So, what's making you procrastinate? Which of your key result areas is your weakest? Take a minute to look back at your key result areas. Grade each of them on a 1-10 scale, with 10 being your greatest strength.

	Key Result Area	Grade
1		
2		
3		
4		
5		
6		
7		

3. Everybody has weaknesses. With yours identified clearly, set goals. Make a plan to become very good in each of your "problem" areas. What is one thing you can do, right now, to work on your weak spots? Use the space here to mind-storm ideas.

Goal: _____

1. _____

_____

_____

2. _____

_____

_____

3. _____

_____

_____

4. _____

_____

_____

5. _____

_____

_____

6. _____

_____

_____

8

Apply the Law of Three

Most of the value that you contribute to your workplace or organization comes from three core tasks. How well you are able to identify these cores tasks and then devote the majority of your time to them determines whether or not you perform at your best.

1. Stop. Set a timer for 30 seconds.

   Start the timer, and write down the three most important tasks that you do in your work. Ready? Go!

   1. _____

   _____

   2. _____

   _____

   3. _____

   _____

2. Next, take a minute to rate yourself, using a 1-10 scale (with 1 as the worst and 10 as the best), in each of these three areas. Give the same task to your boss and other stakeholders.

	Task	Rating
1		
2		
3		

	Task	Rating
1		
2		
3		

	Task	Rating
1		
2		
3		

3. For life outside of work, give yourself 30 seconds for each of the following questions:

What are your three most important *family or relationship* goals right now?

1. _____

2. _____

3. _____

What are your three most important *financial* goals right now?

1. _____

2. _____

3. _____

What are your three most important *health* goals right now?

1. _____

2. _____

3. _____

What are your three most important *personal and professional development* goals right now?

1. _____

2. _____

3. _____

What are your three most important *social and community* goals right now?

1. _____

2. _____

3. _____

What are your three biggest *problems or concerns* in life right now?

1. _____

2. _____

3. _____

4. Once you have identified your three most important goals in each area of your life, organize them by priority. Make plans for their accomplishment, and work on your plans every single day. You will be amazed at what you achieve in the months and years ahead.

1. _____

2. _____

3. _____

9

Prepare Thoroughly Before You Begin

The most creative people in the world set up a work area where they enjoy spending time. Like getting everything ready to cook a great meal—a big, juicy frog, perhaps— getting your work space in order is one of the best ways to beat procrastination and get more things done faster.

1. For now, take a break from writing in this book. Instead, take a minute to clear off your desk. Set up your work area so that it's comfortable, attractive, and conducive to working for long periods. Make sure that your chair is comfortable and that it supports your back and lets your feet sit flat on the floor. Go ahead; I'll wait.

2. Next, put everything that you need to accomplish your most important task—writing materials, login numbers, access codes, and anything else—in easy reach. Put everything you don't need to accomplish this task somewhere out of sight.

3. Take five minutes at the end of the day to get your work area set for tomorrow. Resolve to keep your desk and work space completely cleaned, so you feel effective, efficient, and ready to go whenever you sit down to work. If it helps you remember, set a calendar alert or use some other method to build this into your schedule.

When Shane gets home at night, her bedroom is a total mess. There are files from her day job strewn about, and boxes and packaging materials for her chocolate business stacked to the ceiling in one corner, not to mention all of her books and school materials. Shane decided two things: (1) to leave work at work and (2) to leave nothing on her desk at night, except for those items she would use first thing in the morning.

10

Take It One Oil Barrel at a Time

What's the best way to eat the biggest frogs? One bite at a time. One of the greatest ways to beat procrastination is to focus on a single action you can take, instead of letting yourself get overwhelmed by a huge task. Go as far as you can see. Then you'll be able to see far enough to keep going.

1. Think about the biggest frog in your life right now—personally, professionally, financially. Maybe you're trying to save to buy a house, or anxious about starting a huge project at work. Whatever the frog, make a list of all the steps you need to take to eventually eat that frog.

1. _____

_____

_____

2. _____

_____

_____

3. _____

_____

_____

4. _____

_____

_____

5. _____

_____

_____

6. _____

_____

_____

7. _____

_____

_____

8. _____

_____

_____

9. _____

_____

_____

10. _____

_____

_____

2. Now, take one step immediately. Whatever the first step on your list is, take it. Don't worry about getting everything perfect at first, or get overwhelmed by the enormity of the task as a whole. Just keep focused on that first step.

11

Upgrade Your Key Skills

Continuous learning is the minimum requirement for success in any field—and everything is learnable. The more you learn and know, the more confident and motivated you become. The better you become, the more capable you will be of doing even more.

1. Identify the key skills that can best help you achieve better and faster results. Then highlight those where you have special talents. Among that group, focus even further on those that you enjoy. Use the following diagram to find the overlap among skills, talents, and enjoyment, and focus on them. This is the key to unlocking your personal potential.

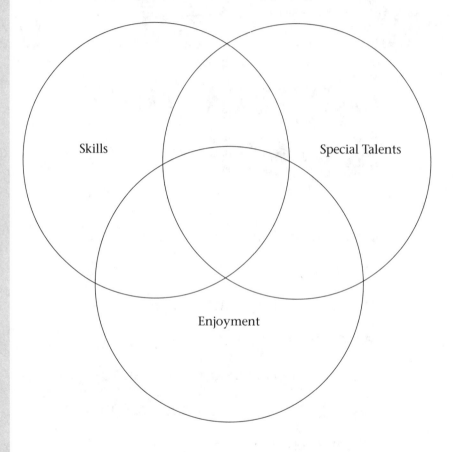

Skills

Special Talents

Enjoyment

2. With areas to focus on in sight, compile a list of media that will help you grow in each area. Research important books or magazines in your field—ones that contain information that can help you become more effective and productive at what you do—and read for at least an hour every day. Also, turn your commute into an opportunity for growth by compiling a list of audiobooks and podcasts. You can become one of the smartest, most capable, and highest-paid people in your field simply by listening to educational audio programs as you travel from place to place.

Books and Periodicals	Podcasts, Audiobooks, and Radio Shows

3. To keep improving, rub elbows with the best minds in your field. Take every course and seminar available on the key skills that can help you. Do some research around conventions and business meetings in your profession or occupation, and use the calendar here to sketch out your next year of in-person learning.

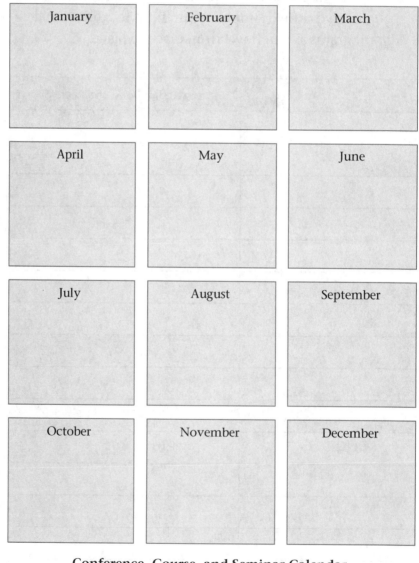

January	February	March
April	May	June
July	August	September
October	November	December

Conference, Course, and Seminar Calendar

Identify Your Key Constraints

Between you and your goals, there is always at least one major constraint to overcome. Whatever you have to do, there is always a limiting factor—the thing that determines how quickly and well you get it done. Whatever your goal or objective, study the task, identify the limiting factor, and focus all your energies on alleviating the bottleneck.

1. What is your most important goal in life today? If you achieved one goal that would have the greatest positive effect on your life, what would it be? What single career accomplishment would have the best effect on your professional life? Write that goal in the circle.

2. Now, think about the things that keep you from achieving that goal. What constraints—internal or external—set the speed at which you accomplish this goal? Where are the choke points?

Goal:

_____

_____

_____

_____

Goal

choke point

Choke points:

1. _____

_____

2. _____

_____

3. _____

_____

3. Identify your key constraint in each area, then focus on removing it.

BUSINESS AND CAREER: What is your single most important goal in your business life?

_____

_____

_____

    a. What is the key INTERNAL constraint that determines how fast you can achieve this goal?

_____

_____

_____

    b. What can you do more of or less of, start or stop, to relieve or ELIMINATE this constraint?

_____

_____

_____

    c. What is the key EXTERNAL constraint that determines how fast you can achieve this goal?

_____

_____

_____

d. What can you do more of or less of, start or stop to relieve or ELIMINATE this constraint?

_____

_____

_____

FAMILY AND RELATIONSHIPS: What is your single most important goal with your family?

_____

_____

_____

a. What is the key INTERNAL constraint that determines how fast you can achieve this goal?

_____

_____

_____

b. What can you do more of or less of, start or stop, to relieve or ELIMINATE this constraint?

_____

_____

_____

c. What is the key EXTERNAL constraint that determines how fast you can achieve this goal?

_____

_____

_____

d. What can you do more of or less of, start or stop, to relieve or ELIMINATE this constraint?

_____

_____

_____

MONEY AND INVESTMENTS: What is your single most important goal regarding your money and investments?

_____

_____

_____

a. What is the key INTERNAL constraint that determines how fast you can achieve this goal?

_____

_____

_____

b. What can you do more of or less of, start or stop, to relieve or ELIMINATE this constraint?

_____

c. What is the key EXTERNAL constraint that determines how fast you can achieve this goal?

_____

_____

_____

d. What can you do more of or less of, start or stop, to relieve or ELIMINATE this constraint?

_____

_____

_____

HEALTH AND FITNESS: What is your single most important health goal?

_____

_____

_____

a. What is the key INTERNAL constraint that determines how fast you can achieve this goal?

_____

_____

_____

b. What can you do more of or less of, start or stop, to relieve or ELIMINATE this constraint?

_____

_____

_____

c. What is the key EXTERNAL constraint that determines how fast you can achieve this goal?

_____

_____

_____

d. What can you do more of or less of, start or stop, to relieve or ELIMINATE this constraint?

_____

_____

_____

What one action are you going to take as a result of your answers to this constraint analysis?

_____

_____

_____

For Shane, the biggest choke point in her life seemed to be time in general—she needed to go to work each day, she needed to put time into class and course work, and her business needed her. But her business, it turned out, didn't always need her to be the one working to grow. Shane decided to take some of the proceeds from her weekly farmers market sales to hire an assistant—a person to work the counter at the farmers market and to deal with some admin work during the week. With the time that freed up, Shane looked into traveling to some trade shows, and spent time she used to spend actually selling chocolate visiting with different retailers in town. In no time, she was selling her wares in dozens of stores.

13

Put the Pressure on Yourself

A very small portion of the population can work without supervision, and those people are leaders. This is the kind of person you are meant to be—and can be—if you decide to be. Get in the habit of putting pressure on yourself; see yourself as a role model and raise your own bar.

1. Congratulations! You have just received a phone call letting you know that you've won an all-expense-paid vacation to the tropical destination of your choice. But there's one catch: you have to leave tomorrow. In this scenario, what would you need to finish today to be able to take the vacation? Set a timer for 60 seconds and write down whatever it is you need to get done, stat!

1. _____

_____

_____

2. _____

_____

_____

3. _____

_____

_____

4. _____

_____

_____

5. _____

_____

_____

6. _____

_____

_____

2. The tropical vacation scenario (or one like it) works great for short-term projects. For longer-term ones, set deadlines and subdeadlines for every task and activity on your to-do list. Use the chart to organize your time for some longer-term goals.

Goal 1:

Deadline:

Task 1:

Subdeadline:

Task 2:

Subdeadline:

Task 3:

Subdeadline:

Goal 2:

Deadline:

Task 1:

Subdeadline:

Task 2:

Subdeadline:

Task 3:

Subdeadline:

3. Even better: make a game out of it! Take one major project on your horizon and write out every step before you begin. Figure out how long each step should take you, then try to beat those time estimates. Imagine someone else is racing you, and resolve to win!

Project:		
Task	**Estimated Time**	**Actual Time**

14

Motivate Yourself into Action

To avoid procrastination, you've got to stay motivated. To stay motivated, become your own personal cheerleader. Know that optimism is the most important quality that you can develop for both personal and professional success and happiness, and strive toward optimism.

1. Most of your emotions, whether they're positive or negative or in-between, are affected by the way you talk to yourself and interpret things throughout the day. If you tell yourself you're no good, guess what? You'll probably feel like you're no good—and then maybe even start acting like it. Nip those negative thoughts in the bud.

   When you look in the mirror, what do you see? Take five minutes to fill the mirror with all the positives you can think of. If you run out of room on the mirror, write down more positive emotions around the mirror.

1. _____

2. _____

3. _____

4. _____

5. _____

6. _____

2. Think of a time something went terribly wrong. It could have been a work-related failure, trouble in your personal life, or anything that would lend itself easily to negativity.

   a. Now, *look for the good* in that situation. No matter what went wrong, what was good or beneficial about it?

      1. _____

         _____

         _____

         _____

         _____

         _____

   b. Optimists believe that each setback and obstacle holds a valuable lesson—one you can use to learn and grow. So, *what was the valuable lesson in your setback?*

      1. _____

         _____

         _____

         _____

         _____

         _____

   c. If you were back in that tough spot, what would you do differently? Optimists *look for the solution to every problem* instead of pouting or getting angry when things don't go as planned. What could you have done, immediately, to solve the problem? What would an ideal next step have been?

1. _____

_____

_____

_____

_____

_____

d. No matter what, optimists *think and talk continually about their goals*. They don't get stuck in the past. So, taking with you what you learned from that difficult situation, where are you going now?

1. _____

_____

_____

_____

_____

_____

15

Technology Is a Terrible Master

Technology can be a powerful tool, but it can also be a drain on your mental energy, and a source of procrastination in and of itself. Don't be chained to your smartphone! Take the time to declutter, detox, and recharge.

1. First things first: declutter. Instead of allowing yourself to be tossed about in a torrent of e-mail and other digital communication, take control. Just because someone sends you an e-mail doesn't mean that he or she owns a piece of your life. Use the checklist below to declutter.

Digital Decluttering Checklist

☐ Unsubscribe to all unwanted newsletters and other mass e-mails. If you get notifications from social media outlets, go into those accounts and stop them from sending you e-mail.

_____ Date Completed

☐ Go into your e-mail account and put up an auto-reply that says something like, "Thanks for writing. I only check e-mail twice per day. If this is an emergency, call."

_____ Date Completed

☐ Clean up the junk! Have a bunch of e-mail that doesn't relate to important goals or relationships? Delete. Delete. Delete. Resolve to delete or ignore all e-mails that don't have a direct impact on you right now.

_____ Date Completed

Just like that, your e-mail volume will shrink drastically, and you'll be far less likely to be overwhelmed by something as silly as e-mail.

2. Build "zones of silence" into your daily routine. Instead of reaching for your phone first thing when you wake up,

turn off your phone and computer for the first hour of the day. Try this again for one hour in the afternoon. Resolve to turn off your phone during meals or other important times with family. Use the form below to plan and commit to your daily detox.

Daily Detox Plan

I will not use technology—smartphone, computer, or other web-connected device—during the following times:

Morning:
from _____ until _____

Lunch:
from _____ until _____

Afternoon:
from _____ until _____

Dinner:
from _____ until _____

No more technology after _____ at night.

3. Unplugging for an hour here and there during the day is great. But to really recharge, you need to unplug for at least one full day each week. Give your mental batteries time to recharge. Use the weekly calendar forms to block out which day each week your own personal blockout will occur!

Sunday	Monday	Tuesday	Wednesday	Thursday	Friday	Saturday

Sunday	Monday	Tuesday	Wednesday	Thursday	Friday	Saturday

Sunday	Monday	Tuesday	Wednesday	Thursday	Friday	Saturday

Sunday	Monday	Tuesday	Wednesday	Thursday	Friday	Saturday

Shane realized that her phone was taking over her life. Every e-mail ping and text message was pulling her away from tasks that urgently needed her attention—and she didn't have that time to share with some computer in her pocket. She decided to take one whole day off from screens each week and to set aside the first hour of her morning and the last hour of her evening to be completely without her phone.

16

Technology Is a Wonderful Servant

Technology can be full of great, productivity-increasing tools. It can also be one of the greatest contributors to distraction and procrastination. Instead of falling prey to technology-as-master, get your technology under control. Make it work for you.

1. What gets in your way? When it comes to technology, we've all been derailed at least once or twice—by social media or some other force for distraction. What are your most frequent temptations? What pulls you away from the things that can really help you succeed? Rank your worst digital distractions.

   1. _____

      _____

      _____

   2. _____

      _____

      _____

   3. _____

      _____

      _____

   4. _____

      _____

      _____

2. Just as you cleaned up your physical work area to set the stage for success, organize your digital space to best position yourself to succeed. Use this checklist to help you best take control of your communication.

Take Control of Your Communication Checklist

☐ Close every program that you don't need for the immediate task at hand. Just as having too many processes running can slow down your machine, it can also pull your attention in every direction but the one where it needs to be focused.

_____ Date Completed

☐ Block the websites that distract you the most. Getting tied up in Twitter? Block it. Floundering in Facebook? Block it. Use the list you created earlier to help you choose what to block.

_____ Date Completed

☐ If all the Internet's a time-sucking rabbit hole, download and install an app that blocks the whole Internet. Whatever you need to do to keep yourself focused on the task at hand, do it.

_____ Date Completed

☐ Show your smartphone that it's not the boss of you. Disable all notifications. Doing so allows you to check your messages on your own schedule—not on its schedule.

_____ Date Completed

☐ Create a phone number, e-mail address, or other method of communication that is reserved only for emergencies. Give it only to your loved ones or appropriate caregivers. Turn off all other channels.

_____ Date Completed

☐ Give your boss or important clients a way to reach you that nobody else has. Or set up your e-mail to sort e-mails from important clients into a "read first" folder.

_____ Date Completed

☐ Schedule large time blocks on your calendar for task completion, just as you would important appointments.

_____ Date Completed

17

Focus Your Attention

Multitasking is a myth. Instead of tackling multiple tasks at once, as the term suggests, people who "multitask" are really shifting their attention. Each time you break your focus—for e-mail, or to respond to a buzz or ping or icon changing color on your phone—it takes significant time to shift your focus back. Don't be a slave to bells and whistles.

1. E-mail and other notifications can be addictive—literally. When you get a new notification, your brain gets a hit of dopamine—a chemical in a lot of drugs, including cocaine. Don't start your day with a hit of dopamine. Instead, resolve to work for 90-minute blocks, and check e-mail only during specific windows. Use the daily schedule on these two pages to plan out your day.

Morning		
Time	**Block**	**Specific Tasks**
Before work	Plan your day	
	90 minutes of work	
15-minute break		
	90 minutes of work	
Check e-mail		
Lunch		

Afternoon		
Time	**Block**	**Specific Tasks**
	90 minutes of work	
15-minute break		
	90 minutes of work	
Check e-mail		
	90 minutes of work	

2. Beyond blocking out your time, always keep your goals of success and high productivity in mind. Before you do anything, ask yourself, "Is this helping me achieve one of my most important goals, or is this just a distraction?"

Which of your daily tasks are really helping you achieve your most important goals?

1. _____

_____

_____

_____

_____

Which tasks are holding you back? Which are just distractions?

1. _____

_____

_____

_____

_____

Resolve to stop taking part in those tasks that are just distractions, for the sake of the tasks that are helping you achieve your goals.

18

Slice and Dice the Task

Don't try to eat big frogs in one bite—you may just choke! Instead, break large tasks up into bite-size morsels. Beyond breaking up large tasks, develop within yourself a compulsion to closure. The more tasks you complete, the better and more elated you'll feel—and the greater the jolt of personal power and energy you'll get.

1. One approach to making large projects feel more manageable is the "salami slice" method. Instead of succumbing to the temptation to tackle the whole thing at once, lay out the task in detail, writing down every step of the task in order. Then resolve to do *just one slice at a time*. As you finish, move on to the next one.

Whole Salami	Slices

2. For larger projects—say, projects that will take weeks or months to complete—try the "Swiss cheese" method. Say you're writing a book or working on some other enormous project. Instead of balking at the enormity of the task, commit to picking away at a piece of it, every day—drill holes in it, like holes in a block of Swiss cheese.

What are some big projects that you could pick away at, over time?

1. _____

_____

_____

_____

_____

_____

Once you've identified them, choose the one with the greatest potential to increase your success. Set aside some time each day to devote to it.

Shane felt like she had a good handle on her day job. When she was there, she put her head down and knocked out everything she had to finish. And with her new assistant really blooming and taking on new tasks, she also felt like her chocolate business was in great shape. But her schoolwork, well, it was getting a little bit neglected. She had this one huge paper due at the end of the semester, and it hung over her head like a dark cloud. Instead of letting it get the best of her or overwhelm her with its size, she decided to break it into pieces. She put 60 minutes of time into research and writing each day. By the time the paper was due, she had been finished with it for two weeks.

19

Create Large Chunks of Time

One of the keys to high levels of performance and productivity is making every minute count. Continuously be thinking of different ways you can save, schedule, and consolidate large chunks of time. Schedule specific activities in preplanned time slots all day long, then build your work around accomplishing key tasks, one at a time.

1. Successful salespeople block off a certain amount of time each day to make calls. Many executives also set aside time blocks to call customers directly or answer correspondence.

What tasks that you need to regularly tackle can you consolidate into regular, scheduled time blocks?

1. _____

_____

_____

2. _____

_____

_____

3. _____

_____

_____

4. _____

_____

_____

5. _____

_____

_____

6. _____

_____

_____

How might you work these sorts of recurring tasks into your regular schedule? Write down triggers and other ways you can do this.

1. _____

_____

_____

_____

_____

_____

2. A time planner can help you visualize blocks of time. It is one of the most powerful tools you have in your battle against procrastination. Use the planner on these four pages, or one like it, to block off time for specific tasks.

Weekly Planner for:			
Time	Monday	Tuesday	Wednesday
8:00			
8:15			
8:30			
8:45			
9:00			
9:15			
9:30			
9:45			
10:00			
10:15			
10:30			
10:45			
11:00			
11:15			
11:30			
11:45			
12:00			

Thursday	Friday	Saturday	Sunday

Time	Monday	Tuesday	Wednesday
12:15			
12:30			
12:45			
1:00			
1:15			
1:30			
1:45			
2:00			
2:15			
2:30			
2:45			
3:00			
3:15			
3:30			
3:45			
4:00			
4:15			
4:30			
4:45			
5:00			

Thursday	Friday	Saturday	Sunday

20

Develop a Sense of Urgency

Highly productive people are action oriented—they take the time to think, plan, and set goals, but they also take immediate action. Working on important tasks quickly and continually can trigger "flow"—an amazing mental state where you feel clear, elated, calm, and effective. Instead of continually talking about what you're going to do, take immediate action, and you'll be more likely to trigger flow in yourself.

1. In areas where you have a tendency to procrastinate, what is it that keeps you from getting started?

   1. _____

   _____

   _____

   _____

   _____

   _____

   What is the one area where you find yourself having the strongest tendency to procrastinate?

   1. _____

   _____

2. One of the simplest and most effective ways to get started on unpleasant tasks—or just tasks that seem easy to put off—is to repeat the words "Do it now!" to yourself. When you catch yourself getting off task, it can help to repeat the words "Back to work!" to yourself.

Cut out the reminders below and tack them up in places where you will see them all the time—or wherever you go to procrastinate.

Do it now!

Do it now!

Do it now!

Do it now!

3. You know what to do with these: cut them out, hang them up, then get back to work.

Back to work!

Back to work!

Back to work!

Back to work!

21

Single Handle Every Task

Single handling means that once you have started a task, you keep working on it until it is complete. Each time you get off task, the task takes longer to complete—as much as 500 percent longer. The more you discipline yourself to work nonstop on a single task, the more and better quality work you get done in less and less time.

1. In the end, success requires large amounts of self-discipline. By focusing on your more valuable tasks until completion, you build good habits—you become a better person.

Use the space below to pledge to yourself that once you start your most important task, you'll work until you finish it, without distraction or diversion.

I promise to . . .

Shane kept finding herself losing steam at the end of the day. "Ah, I'll finish it tomorrow," she'd say, instead of powering through the last little bit of her schoolwork. This meant that she had to start at the same place the next day, wasting valuable time she could have been devoting to the next important task. Instead, she decided never to end a day midtask. She hung up a big "Do it now!" sign over her desk and a "Back to work!" tag on her TV, each nudging her in the right direction when the temptation to call it quits early was strong.

Conclusion:
Putting It All Together

Here is a summary of the 21 great ways to stop procrastinating and get more things done faster. Review these rules and principles regularly until they become firmly ingrained in your thinking and actions, and your future will be guaranteed.

1. **Set the table:** Decide exactly what you want. Clarity is essential. Write out your goals and objectives before you begin.

2. **Plan every day in advance:** Think on paper. Every minute you spend in planning can save you 5 or 10 minutes in execution.

3. **Apply the 80/20 Rule to everything:** Twenty percent of your activities will account for 80 percent of your results. Always concentrate your efforts on that top 20 percent.

4. **Consider the consequences:** Your most important tasks and priorities are those that can have the most serious consequences, positive or negative, on your life or work. Focus on these above all else.

5. **Practice creative procrastination:** Since you can't do everything, you must learn to deliberately put off those tasks that are of low value so that you have enough time to do the few things that really count.

6. **Use the ABCDE Method continually:** Before you begin work on a list of tasks, take a few moments to organize them by value and priority so you can be sure of working on your most important activities.

7. **Focus on key result areas:** Identify those results that you absolutely, positively have to achieve to do your job well, and work on them all day long.

8. **Apply the law of three:** Identify the three things you do in your work that account for 90 percent of your contribution, and focus on getting them done before anything else. You will then have more time for your family and personal life.

9. **Prepare thoroughly before you begin:** Have everything you need at hand before you start. Assemble all the papers, information, tools, work materials, and numbers you might require so that you can get started and keep going.

10. **Take it one oil barrel at a time:** You can accomplish the biggest and most complicated job if you just complete it one step at a time.

11. **Upgrade your key skills:** The more knowledgeable and skilled you become at your key tasks, the faster you start them and the sooner you get them done. Determine exactly what it is that you are very good at doing, or could be very good at, and throw your whole heart into doing those specific things very, very well.

12. **Identify your key constraints:** Determine the bottlenecks or choke points, internal or external, that set the speed at which you achieve your most important goals, and focus on alleviating them.

13. **Put the pressure on yourself:** Imagine that you have to leave town for a month, and work as if you had to get your major task completed before you left.

14. **Motivate yourself into action:** Be your own cheerleader. Look for the good in every situation. Focus on the solution rather than the problem. Always be optimistic and constructive.

15. **Technology is a terrible master:** Take back your time from enslaving technological addictions. Learn to often turn things off and leave them off.

16. **Technology is a wonderful servant:** Make your technological tools confront you with what is most important and protect you from what is least important.

17. **Focus your attention:** Stop the interruptions and distractions that interfere with completing your most important tasks.

18. **Slice and dice the task:** Break large, complex tasks down into bite-size pieces, and then do just one small part of the task to get started.

19. **Create large chunks of time:** Organize your days around large blocks of time so you can concentrate for extended periods on your most important tasks.

20. **Develop a sense of urgency:** Make a habit of moving fast on your key tasks. Become known as a person who does things quickly and well.

21. **Single handle every task:** Set clear priorities, start immediately on your most important task, and then work without stopping until the job is 100 percent complete. This is the real key to high performance and maximum personal productivity.

Make a decision to practice these principles every day until they become second nature to you. With these habits of personal management as a permanent part of your personality, your future success will be unlimited.

Just do it! *Eat that frog!*

As she hangs her MBA on the wall of her new office, Shane smiles with satisfaction. It's been a challenging couple of years, but she feels good about what she has accomplished—finishing all her course work, and growing her chocolate business to the point where she no longer needs her old day job. Suddenly, the phone rings, shattering her moment of silent introspection. "Back to work," she says to herself with a grin, and answers the phone. There is still much to do—and there are many, many frogs to eat.

Digital Resources

You may prefer to work on some of the exercises in this workbook in a digital format or print them as PDFs to fill out multiple times. If so, go to www .bkconnection.com/ETFworkbook (use the code ETF21ACTION). Free charts and graphs included in the Digital Resources are daily activity lists, a weekly planner, a monthly calendar, and reminder notes.

Learning Resources of Brian Tracy International

Brian Tracy
SPEAKER, TRAINER, SEMINAR LEADER

Brian Tracy is one of the top professional speakers in the world, addressing more than 250,000 people each year throughout the United States, Europe, Asia, and Australia.

Brian's keynote speeches, talks, and seminars are described as "inspiring, entertaining, informative, and motivational." His audiences include Fortune 500 companies and every size of business and association.

Book Brian today to speak on one of the following topics:

Business Model Reinvention—How to grow your sales and profitability in any market by analyzing and improving your business model.

High Performance Selling—How to outthink, outperform, and outsell your competition using the most advanced strategies and tactics known to modern selling.

Maximum Achievement—How the top people think and act in every area of personal and business life. Countless practical, proven methods and strategies for peak performance.

Leadership in the 21st Century—How to apply the most powerful leadership principles to manage, motivate, and get better results, faster than ever before.

Brian will carefully customize his talk for you and for your needs. Visit Brian Tracy International at http://www.briantracy.com/speaking/ for more information on how to book Brian for your next event.

Brian Tracy's Online Training Programs—The Keys to Ultimate Success in Any Area of Your Life

Power Productivity with Brian Tracy

If you enjoyed the timeless lessons in *Eat That Frog!*, be sure to check out Power Productivity, Brian Tracy's online training and certification course for time management mastery. This course is designed for those who want to learn, develop, or improve their time management skill set so they can maximize their productivity and achieve greater success in every aspect of life.

To learn more about Power Productivity with Brian Tracy, visit www.briantracy.com/powerproductivity.

Goals Mastery for Personal and Financial Achievement

If you're looking to make true change in your life, consider Goals Mastery for Personal and Financial Achievement, Brian Tracy's ninety-day transformational program that provides you with the clarity and confidence you need to dissolve self-imposed limitations and become an unequivocal powerhouse in the pursuit of your biggest, most important dreams.

To learn more about Goals Mastery for Personal and Financial Achievement, visit www.briantracy.com/goalsmastery achievement.

How to Write a Book and Become a Published Author

According to Amazon, 82 percent of Americans want to write a book, which is why Brian created his virtual training course, How to Write a Book and Become a Published Author. Using the proven, four-step process that Brian has used to write over seventy of his own books, this program shares an easy-to-follow system for aspiring authors to write and publish their first book.

To learn more about How to Write a Book and Become a Published Author, visit www.briantracy.com/howtowriteabook.

The 6-Figure Speaker

The 6-Figure Speaker is an all-encompassing training course for developing and mastering the art of professional speaking developed by Brian Tracy. This eighteen-part virtual training course is delivered over two consecutive weeks through a sequence of online video modules delivered daily. The course covers everything from powerful speech preparation methods and techniques for overcoming fear to vocal techniques and strategies for negotiating speaker contracts.

To learn more about Brian Tracy's 6-Figure Speaker online virtual training program, visit www.briantracy.com /6figurespeaker.

21st Century Sales Training for Elite Performance

Becoming a master at selling is the single greatest skill you can develop to achieve your personal, professional, and financial goals, which is why Brian created his sales training program, 21st Century Sales Training for Elite Performance. This sales training course is for anyone who wants to move to the top of his or her field, close more sales, make more money, and gain the respect of peers and colleagues as a leader in sales.

To learn more about Brian Tracy's 21st Century Sales Training for Elite Performance program, visit www.briantracy.com /21stcentury.

About the Author

 Brian Tracy is one of the top business speakers in the world today. He has designed and presented seminars for more than 1,000 large companies and more than 10,000 small and medium-sized enterprises in 75 countries on the subjects of Leadership, Management, Professional Selling, Business Model Reinvention, and Profit Improvement. He has addressed more than 5,000,000 people in more than 5,000 talks and presentations worldwide. He currently speaks to 250,000 people per year. His fast-moving, entertaining video-based training programs are taught in 38 countries.

Brian is a bestselling author. He has written more than 80 books that have been translated into 42 languages, including *Kiss That Frog!, Find Your Balance Point, Goals!, Flight Plan, Maximum Achievement, No Excuses!, Advanced Selling Strategies,* and *How the Best Leaders Lead.* He is happily married, with four children and five grandchildren. He is the president of Brian Tracy International and lives in Solana Beach, California. He can be reached at briantracy@briantracy.com.

Don't put if off! You've got the workbook, now get the book!

Eat That Frog!

21 Great Ways to Stop Procrastinating and Get More Done in Less Time

Now in it's third edition, *Eat That Frog!* is one of the bestselling time management books in the world—it's sold over 1.6 million copies worldwide and has been translated into over 40 languages, from Arabic to Vietnamese.

Brian Tracy offers 21 clear, concise ways to accomplish your goals in record time, easily and efficiently. He cuts to the core of what is vital to effective time management: decision, discipline, and determination. In this fully revised and updated edition, Tracy adds two new chapters. The first explains how you can use technology to remind yourself of what is most important and protect yourself from what is least important. The second offers advice for maintaining focus in our era of constant distractions, electronic and otherwise.

This life-changing book will ensure that you get more of your important tasks done—today!

Paperback, 144 pages, ISBN 978-1-62656-941-6
PDF ebook ISBN 978-1-62656-942-3
ePub ebook ISBN 978-1-62656-943-0
Digital audiobook ISBN 978-1-62656-944-7

Berrett–Koehler Publishers, Inc.
www.bkconnection.com

800.929.2929

Eat That Frog! Cards

Designed for individual or group play, these cards offer a fun, hands-on way to identify what's holding you back and develop the right strategies to stop procrastinating and get more done.

One set of cards in the deck describes procrastination habits, which you rank in order of importance. Do you become paralyzed by the length of your to-do list? Do you work on simple but low-impact tasks first and neglect the harder, higher-impact tasks? Are you too easily distracted by social media?

Once you've ranked your negative habits, you then match these "problem" cards with "solution" cards that describe strategies for overcoming them. You'll end up with a comprehensive, memorable, and personalized guide to dealing with your biggest behavioral obstacles to success.

Box with 56 cards and instruction sheet
ISBN 978-1-5230-8469-2

Berrett–Koehler Publishers, Inc.
www.bkconnection.com/frogs   **800.929.2929**

Eat That Frog! Video Training Program

It's like getting a private coaching session from one of the world's leading success experts! In this video training program, Brian Tracy presents the lessons of *Eat That Frog!* in a casual setting, sitting right across the desk from you. The 2.5-hour course features twenty-three segments: a special introduction, all twenty-one chapters from *Eat That Frog!*, and an inspiring conclusion.

Each segment invites viewers to reinforce what they've learned using exercises in the *Eat That Frog! Action Workbook* so that good habits truly get a chance to sink in. Viewers can engage in the course at their own pace and by the end will have the tools to stop procrastinating and get more done—once and for all!

150 minutes
DVD, ISBN 978-1-52309-450-9
Download, ISBN 978-1-5230-9451-6
Streaming, ISBN 978-1-5230-9452-3

Berrett–Koehler Publishers, Inc.
www.bkconnection.com/frogs

800.929.2929

Eat That Frog! Audiobook

Absorb the lessons of *Eat That Frog!* in the car, at the gym, or on the couch; while cooking, cleaning, gardening, or waiting in line—anywhere you like! Read by Brian Tracy, this audiobook can be downloaded to any device. So you can listen on your phone, your tablet, your laptop, or your desktop—a great example of making technology a wonderful servant, as Brian recommends in chapter 16. Turn your slack time into learning time! Use your ears to eat those frogs!

MP3 digital audiobook, 150 minutes, ISBN 978-1-62656-944-7
Audio CD ISBN 978-1-52007-199-2
MP3 CD ISBN 978-1-52007-200-5
CDs available for purchase from Dreamscape at 877.983.7326

Berrett–Koehler Publishers, Inc.
www.bkconnection.com/frogs   **800.929.2929**

Free Full-Color Sticker!

Make sure you stick to your goals! This bright and colorful 4-inch-diameter sticker is perfect for your laptop, day planner, notebook, refrigerator, office—any place you want to be reminded to tackle your most important tasks first!

To get your free sticker, just go to
www.bkconnection.com/frogsticker

BK® Berrett–Koehler Publishers, Inc.
www.bkconnection.com/frogs

800.929.2929

Also by Brian Tracy

Be a Sales Superstar
21 Great Ways to Sell More, Faster, Easier in Tough Markets

Based on his close work with top sales-people and his keen observation of their methods, as well as his own experiences as a record-breaking salesman, Brian Tracy presents key ideas and techniques that address both the *inner* game of selling (the mental component) and the *outer* game of selling (the methods and techniques of actually making the sale).

Paperback, 168 pages, ISBN 978-1-57675-273-9
PDF ebook, ISBN 978-1-60509-836-4
ePub ebook, ISBN 978-1-60509-694-0

Goals!
How to Get Everything You Want—Faster Than You Ever Thought Possible, Second Edition

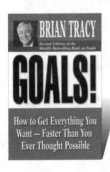

Brian Tracy presents a simple, powerful, and effective system for setting and achieving goals—a method that has been used by more than one million people to achieve extraordinary things. In this revised and expanded second edition, he has added three new chapters addressing areas in which goals can be most rewarding but also the toughest to set and keep: finances, family, and health.

Paperback, 304 pages, ISBN 978-1-60509-411-3
PDF ebook, ISBN 978-1-60509-412-0
ePub ebook, ISBN 978-1-60509-940-8

Berrett–Koehler Publishers, Inc.
www.bkconnection.com

800.929.2929

Flight Plan
The Real Secret of Success

Life is a journey, and as with any other journey you need clear goals, plans, and schedules to get from where you are now to where you want to be—a flight plan. In this powerful, practical book, Brian Tracy uses the metaphor of an airplane trip to help you chart a course to greater achievement, happiness, and personal fulfillment.

Hardcover, 168 pages, ISBN 978-1-57675-497-9
Paperback, ISBN 978-1-60509-275-1
PDF ebook, ISBN 978-1-57675-556-3
ePub ebook ISBN, 978-1-60994-042-3

The 100 Absolutely Unbreakable Laws of Business Success

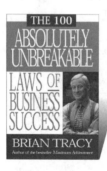

Why are some people more successful in business than others? Why do some businesses flourish where others fail? In this eye-opening practical guide, Brian Tracy presents a set of universal laws that lie behind the success of businesspeople everywhere. He provides numerous real-life examples to illustrate how each law functions and practical guidance and exercises for applying each to your life and work.

Paperback, 336 pages, ISBN 978-1-57675-126-8
PDF ebook, ISBN 978-1-57675-794-9
ePub ebook ISBN 978-1-60509-898-2

Berrett–Koehler Publishers, Inc.
www.bkconnection.com   800.929.2929

Berrett–Koehler
Publishers

Berrett-Koehler is an independent publisher dedicated to an ambitious mission: *Connecting people and ideas to create a world that works for all.*

We believe that the solutions to the world's problems will come from all of us, working at all levels: in our organizations, in our society, and in our own lives. Our BK Business books help people make their organizations more humane, democratic, diverse, and effective (we don't think there's any contradiction there). Our BK Currents books offer pathways to creating a more just, equitable, and sustainable society. Our BK Life books help people create positive change in their lives and align their personal practices with their aspirations for a better world.

All of our books are designed to bring people seeking positive change together around the ideas that empower them to see and shape the world in a new way.

And we strive to practice what we preach. At the core of our approach is Stewardship, a deep sense of responsibility to administer the company for the benefit of all of our stakeholder groups including authors, customers, employees, investors, service providers, and the communities and environment around us. Everything we do is built around this and our other key values of quality, partnership, inclusion, and sustainability.

This is why we are both a B-Corporation and a California Benefit Corporation—a certification and a for-profit legal status that require us to adhere to the highest standards for corporate, social, and environmental performance.

We are grateful to our readers, authors, and other friends of the company who consider themselves to be part of the BK Community. We hope that you, too, will join us in our mission.

A BK Life Book

BK Life books help people clarify and align their values, aspirations, and actions. Whether you want to manage your time more effectively or uncover your true purpose, these books are designed to instigate infectious positive change that starts with you. Make your mark!

To find out more, visit **www.bkconnection.com**.

Berrett–Koehler
Publishers

Connecting people and ideas
to create a world that works for all

Dear Reader,

Thank you for picking up this book and joining our worldwide community of Berrett-Koehler readers. We share ideas that bring positive change into people's lives, organizations, and society.

To welcome you, we'd like to offer you a free e-book. You can pick from among twelve of our bestselling books by entering the promotional code **BKP92E** here: http://www.bkconnection.com/welcome.

When you claim your free e-book, we'll also send you a copy of our e-newsletter, the *BK Communiqué*. Although you're free to unsubscribe, there are many benefits to sticking around. In every issue of our newsletter you'll find

- A free e-book
- Tips from famous authors
- Discounts on spotlight titles
- Hilarious insider publishing news
- A chance to win a prize for answering a riddle

Best of all, our readers tell us, "Your newsletter is the only one I actually read." So claim your gift today, and please stay in touch!

Sincerely,

Charlotte Ashlock
Steward of the BK Website

Questions? Comments? Contact me at bkcommunity@bkpub.com.

Certified
Corporation
bcorporation.net